#WriteYourselfALoveLetterChallenge

Part Journal, Part Manifesto on Becoming Your Best Self

Kia Smith

Copyright © 2021 Kia Smith

ISBN: 9798618713214

All rights reserved. No part of this publication may be reproduced, stored in a retrieval system, or transmitted in any form or by any means – for example, electronic, mechanical, photocopy, recording, or otherwise – without the prior written permission of the copyright holder, except as provided by USA copyright law.

DEDICATION

This book is dedicated to my inner child, who struggled to be heard until she discovered her gift of writing.

This book is dedicated to the woman I once was, who once settled out of conditioning and fear, afraid to love herself and demand better.

This book is dedicated to the woman I currently am.

I love her so much because I fought to become her. This book is dedicated to the woman I am becoming, the work you put in has paid off. This book is dedicated to my little sister Lola, who I pray will not have to endure the same struggles on her own journey of self-love.

This book is dedicated to all the women before me, who have scars from their own journeys yet have the courage to redefine what self-love is to them. This book is dedicated to all of us. May we love ourselves fiercely. Unashamedly. Loudly. Boldly.

Love,

Kia

CONTENTS

DEDICATION..3

CONTENTS..5

FOREWORD...7

How To Use This Book..9

The History..10

1. What is Self-Love?..13
2. Everything starts in childhood...................................29
3. Low Self-Esteem..39
4. Self-Sabotage...49
5. Am I trauma bonding?..57
6. Accountability..65
7. Healing..73
8. Am I Doing This Right?...85
9. What if I never find my person?...............................91
10. Redefining Self-Love..103
11. Your Turn...121

Epilogue..129

About the Author..131

FOREWORD

Dear whoever is reading this,

First things first, I just want to say thank you. It's one thing to create something. It's one thing to share it with others. It's one thing for others to believe in you and your words so much that they buy it, share it and refer back to it time and time again.

When I started this four years ago in the summer of 2016, I had no idea that it would turn into any of this. I was just simply following instructions for a classroom assignment and then boom… It turned into a blog post, a social media challenge, then a workshop.

If you've ever been to a workshop, thank you.

If you've ever publicly or privately written a love letter to yourself, thank you.

If you've ever found yourself fighting to love you just a little bit more each day, thank you.

I never said it would be easy, but it *is* worth it.

Thanks again.

Love,

Kia

Most of us have suffered heartache. Pain has opened us up— given us the opportunity to learn from our suffering— to make ourselves ready for the love that is promised. We know love is there. Some of us are still waiting. We know we will love again. And when we love, we know love will last.

Significantly, we know, having learned through much trial and error, that true love begins with self-love. And that time and time again our search for love brings us back to the place where we started, back to our own heart's mirror, where we can look upon our female selves with love and be renewed.

- bell hooks, The Female Search For Love

How To Use This Book

So in this book, you will read some private and public love letters that I've written to myself over the last few years. Following each letter, there are journal prompt questions that you will be able to read and respond to. Every question does not have to be answered all at once. Feel free to skip around the questions and come back to them when you are ready. At the very end of this book, you will have a chance to write a love letter to yourself. Think of this book as your personal journal where you can jot down answers to the questions. If you have purchased this book via Kindle or another digital format, you might want to keep a spare notebook nearby for the questions so you can answer them later.

The History

As legend has it… okay I'm kidding. Honestly, the history behind *#WriteYourselfALoveLetterChallenge* is quite simple. Summer '16 I was taking a summer class during my undergrad days at SIU. The class was on social media and how people interact with it.

We had a big project: Develop some type of campaign that people could connect with and analyze the ways they connect via social media. Around this time, I had been a blogger for 5 years, and knew that I wanted my blog to be the medium for the campaign. Around that time, Facebook was ripe with different types of "challenges" such as

The Real Hair Challenge, the No Makeup Challenge, Throwback Picture Challenges, etc.

As a blogger, I transitioned my blog from writing strictly about music and hot topics here and there to writing fully about my relationships, my life transitions, and my growing pains. At this moment, my blog transitioned into what is now known as my public diary with an intimate twist.

Summer 2016 was a hard one for me and to be honest, ever since I started dating, I struggled with loving myself, having high self-esteem, and knowing my self worth. And whether they were vocal about it or not, I knew other people around me dealt with the same things I have dealt with. So thinking about those themes led me to create #WriteYourselfALoveLetterChallenge, where basically, you had to post a picture of yourself and write nice things about yourself. You were not allowed to talk down on yourself, mention flaws, etc. You had to give yourself pure love. In front of everyone on the internet.

Sounds easy right? Who doesn't like talking about themselves in a positive manner?

Wrong. For many, this challenge was hard. It was emotional. It was life changing. And at that moment I knew, my transparency, my self-reflection and my resilience would one day help people. This is Write Yourself A Love Letter Challenge, a journal and manifesto on becoming your best self.

1
What is Self-Love?

6.16. 2016

Dear Kia,

> First of all, I must admit how awkward it is to write a letter to myself but even more awkward for me to let everybody and they mama read it LOL. But I created this challenge for a reason, so I must play by the rules.
>
> As you know Kia, this letter comes at a time when you haven't been feeling like yourself. Your energy has been off, you haven't felt loved, you haven't felt inspired or inspiring, you haven't felt pretty enough, you've been feeling used and disrespected. You've been feeling stuck and unappreciated.
>
> But somehow, despite what you may feel, you look at each day as an opportunity to start fresh and new, and that is something I really admire about you Kia.
>
> I love you because your heart and your spirit is one that can transform the world and touch the lives of everyone you come across. I love you because your love is the fire that will ignite anyone, the passion to fulfill any dream and all the words needed to uplift and encourage. You love so openly, yet you protect yourself because you know how fragile and valuable your heart is.
>
> I love you because you're giving. Whether it is a listening ear or aiding someone in need, you give without ill intentions, without throwing it back in someone's face.

You give without conditions and your heart to serve others is boundless.

I love you because you are unafraid to make mistakes and learn from them. Your flaws have made you who you are at this very moment, and they give you a unique story to tell. I love you because you strive to take care of yourself mentally and that you encourage others to do the same. I love you because you are growing to be very unapologetic, and that even when people don't like or agree with who you are, you don't try to please them.

I love you because you seek to define yourself to yourself. You don't allow yourself to be put into boxes, and you embrace how multifaceted you are. I love you because of your complex layers, for they bring you a special surprise each day.

I love your humor. I love the sound of your laugh. I love the lines that form around your mouth when you start smiling, and the way you throw your head back when something is hilarious to you. I love the way your eyes sparkle when you look at people and how brown they are. I love the way your eyelashes curl and I adore the shape of your eyebrows.

I love the way you think and your curious intellect. Not only are you book smart, you are filled with so much wisdom too. I love how you ask questions, how you form your opinions, how open your mind is. If there is one thing that no one can take away from you, it is your ability to think for yourself, regardless of what anyone else is saying.

I love how both introverted and extroverted you can

be.. It means you understand the tranquility of being alone, but you also know the power of being around like minded people.

I love you because you understand how much of a loving, beautiful, and valuable woman you are. I love how you refuse to let anyone or anything stunt your growth, how you won't allow others to mistreat you and how you refuse to settle for less than you deserve. Sometimes its hard for you to believe because you may make the same mistakes over and over again, but then you snap out of it and realize that in life there are truly no mistakes, only lessons learned.

I love how dedicated you are when you truly want to achieve something. You never give up, you keep going no matter how long it takes. You don't wait around on others to anything, you have always had such an independent and innovative spirit.

I love you because you value healthy relationships with both friends and family. I love that you will go above and beyond for them while still holding on to your sanity, yet love them fiercely enough so they don't have to question you. I love how you strive to always love them unconditionally, encourage them and support their dreams.

Speaking of dreams, I love that you believe in the power of your own. The things you want to do in your life will change the hearts and minds of many, but I love that you believe that if you touch at least ONE person, you know that your work matters.

I love how you support others. It literally brings a smile to my face to see how you will show others that you care.

I love your passion and intensity. In a world where so many will force themselves to be robots, I love how you will show your anger, your temper, your love, your sadness... It shows that your heart is working and that you care.

I love how you are constantly growing. You are not the same person from 1 year ago, 5 years ago and I am sure that you will not be the same person 15 years from now.

I love you because you command and demand respect everywhere you go, from everyone you meet. If you are disrespected, I love how unafraid you are to correct that person and go about your day.

I love you because you will always stand up for people and stand up for what is right. No matter if people disagree with you.

I love you because you are working on having a more forgiving heart. It is not easy, but you are trying and I commend you on the effort.

I love you because you are beautiful, but not only because of the way you look. It is more so because of the way you make yourself feel, and how you touch those around you. You are inspiring. Own that. You are inspiring. You may not see it right now, but I see it everyday.

I love you because you know that there is sometimes "good" in goodbye and how you will protect yourself from negative energy by any means necessary. I love how unafraid you are of hard work and how you adapt to change so well.

I love you because you don't let your life's circumstances define who you are, hold you back, or keep you down. Though you've been in some tough situations, you always bounce better than ever before.

I love the fact that you are a writer, and that you know your pen can take you places. I love how you let it describe your feelings, how it has told amazing stories and how it has healed you.

I love you because even in the midst of life's storms, you manage to find peace within you.

I love the woman that you are but I know I will really love the woman that you are becoming..

I love you simply because you are you.

Kia Smith.

Kia Cherrice Joy Smith to be specific.

Filled with sugar, sass, and a whole lot of class.

Who is about as multifaceted as they come and as outspoken as she pleases.

Who loves God and herself.

Who loves herself and others.

I love her. And I love you.

I love you Kia and don't you ever forget it.

Sincerely,

Kia

Self-love isn't something that you just know how to do, you have to learn it. You have to practice it. If you didn't grow up with it, you have to reprogram your mind to accept it, receive it, and channel it all times. Once you grasp the concept of self-love, you then have to fight to keep it. It will be tested.

I've tweaked on myself so many times on this journey of self-love and used to feel so much shame when I made the mistake of not sticking to boundaries and self-sabotaging my peace and happiness. It became so bad that I felt like a fraud. How could I preach the importance of loving yourself when I was failing so miserably at it? It would be a while before I learned that a part of self-love was no longer making myself a prisoner for my past decisions. I deserve forgiveness, compassion, and grace, too.

Time went on and the journey for self-love got deeper. I got less concerned with "doing it right" and more concerned with living my truth authentically. Doing this thang, *authentically*. I never needed to be perfect. Just authentic. Committed to trying again and constantly redefining what it meant to love myself. That's what this journey became.

After writing that, I made choices that made life harder for me. I battled the rest of 2016 in between therapy, mental and emotional breakdowns, shedding layers, and trying my hardest to stick to this journey that I was now dedicated to. A year later, I revisited the challenge and wrote a follow up letter.

6.16. 2017

Dear Kia,

Last year when you wrote this letter, you were personally battling a storm that not too many knew about and you didn't think that you would survive it. Each day was a mental and emotional battle that no one fully understood and while you appeared to be resilient and strong, you struggled to hold on just a little bit longer when you secretly wanted to fall apart.

The year of 2016 was a tough one. You battled some serious issues and fell into a deep abyss of darkness that no one but God, counseling, and yourself could pull you out of.

But you got out. You got your magic back. And I'm so proud of you.

I love you because you are the definition of light. I love you because you are relentless in pursuing your passion, and you are willing to do whatever it takes to manifest your dreams.

I love you because the older you get, the more you grow into yourself. You know who you are. You know what you want. You embrace how multifaceted you are. Every day you look in the mirror and decide that in spite of what you've been through, you know that you are worthy of love, affection, commitment, blessings and every good thing that this world has to offer.

I love you because you constantly try to do the work that goes into being a better person each day. I love you because you have gotten more comfortable with transparency. You know that there is strength in vulnerability, and know that even though it is sometimes difficult, your story must be told.

I love you because you are always willing to grow and learn. You don't confine yourself to only receiving knowledge in a classroom, you seek ways to self-educate and stand firm in your beliefs. I love you because you are passionate, and you exude passion in everything that you do.

I love you because you are human. Yeah, you believe in positive vibes but you also believe in telling people when they have you fucked up. No longer are you that little girl who allows people to walk all over her or who suffers in silence because she is afraid of what people may think or say about her.

I love you because you are humble. You are thankful for all the blessings you receive, and in turn, you do your best to bless others. I love you because you know the importance of lifting others as you climb because you know the power that is in paying it forward.

I love you because you love yourself enough to protect your energy without missing out on meaningful interactions. Your level of discernment has been so high lately and you have started listening to your gut when things don't look, feel, or sound right.

I love you because you know the power of walking away. I love you because you don't let life's circumstances make you bitter. You may have your bad days, but you are not bitter.

I love you because of how you dream. You have million dollar ideas in your head girl. You surprise me all the time with what you come up with.

I love you because you choose to be powerful.

Obviously, I love you for your inner and outer beauty. Your smile still lights up a room. Your hair is a crown of glory. Your shape is to die for. Your personality is unforgettable. You are the peace and calm for many storms, your words empower and connect with many.

I love that you've kept your promise to yourself about writing more in 2017. Not only have you been writing more, but you've been writing some good shit at that! You're growing so much in that area and I am so happy that you have something that makes you happy. It truly warms my heart to see you work on something and bring it to life and then share it with others with the hope that it may motivate, connect and inspire them.

I love how you have overcome so much since last year. You are strength in its highest form.

The woman you are is truly amazing and I will always love you, support you and affirm you every step of the way of your life journey.

I love you because you succeed. Congrats on all your accomplishments and congrats to much more!

I love you because you don't fold for anyone's foolishness. You have mastered the art of loving people from a distance and I couldn't be more proud. You love yourself enough to know who deserves your time and energy and who does not.

I love you because there were a few times last year when you were emotionally suffering and you thought you would never get over it and you thought you wouldn't survive. But one year later and look at you: surviving and shit. ♥

I love everything about you girl, even the "ugly" parts because you are fearfully and wonderfully made. You are perfectly imperfect. You are about as dope as they come.

Here's to another year of reflecting, progressing, and growing into a better woman each day.

Love always and forever,

Kia ♥♥♥

How do you speak to yourself when you repeat the same mistake?

What do you need to forgive yourself for?

How do you show love to yourself *and* still hold yourself accountable?

Are you gentle with yourself?

2
Everything starts in childhood

How does one's sense of self-love get warped anyway? Does it start in childhood? Is it based on the behavior we observe from our parents? Is it after a love connection gone wrong? Truly, what makes us not love ourselves?

If I am to be honest with myself, I wasn't explicitly taught how and why I should love myself. In my early adolescence, I had an emotionally distant relationship with my father. Him and my mother did not have a healthy relationship with each other and as a result, I was often caught in the cross-fire. They didn't love or like each other very much by the time I was born, but trauma bonding and codependency kept them together until my father moved on and my mother had the guts to leave him. I don't remember soft or tender moments between them. I never saw my mother get romantic things done for her by my father, and I never saw my mom be there emotionally for my dad and support his hopes and dreams. This isn't to say that it never happened, but what I am saying is that I never saw it.

I needed my dad a lot back then. We never had sit down talks about boys or love or navigating relationships until I became an adult. I am sure he *wanted* to be there for me emotionally, but due to his own hang ups about emotions, he couldn't. He didn't know how. Should I fault him for that?

It is difficult, navigating a world wanting to be seen and heard by the ones you love, so when you are not, you seek it in other people.

At 12, I started having little boyfriends, obsessing over them. I would daydream about them all the time and write in my diary about the life I imagined for us. Things that I never saw at home and not even on TV really, I just created my own realities. My mama found my diary one day, read it, and was waiting on me when I got home. Perched on the couch, I was gonna breeze past her (after speaking of course) like I usually do and head straight to my room to take off my uniform, but she stopped me dead in my tracks.

She said my name in a tone of voice that I still remember to this day. I answered her, and from what I remember it was a brief talk about boys and the last thing she said to me was "You don't need a man to validate you."

I would spend many years after that learning and relearning that lesson. It is hard, because young women are often socialized from birth until old age that having a man and a family is at the center of what defines you as a woman. The messaging was confusing for me: one minute it's cool to be single and not need the outward validation, the next minute you're in your 20's and everyone is wondering why you're not dating, where ya man is and when you gone have some kids.

    I thought loving myself was enough.

    And it is.

But I still wanted that validation. I still wanted to create those realities I wrote about in my childhood diaries and as a result, I searched for the broken parts of me in other people. Imagine wanting someone to fill your cup when you don't even know how to fill it yourself! I tried to create homes in people who couldn't even reciprocate. Or, they had abandonment/codependency issues of their own so me trying to get my cup filled when they had their own issues was merely a disaster.

    The journey would only get harder from there.

How was the concept of self-love introduced to you in childhood, if it was at all?

What do you remember about your parent's relationship?

Was it healthy or unhealthy?

What factors about their relationship contribute to your belief?

_____

_____

_____

_____

_____

_____

_____

_____

_____

_____

_____

_____

_____

What did your childhood teach you about self-love?

If you didn't learn anything in childhood about self-love, what do you wish you would have learned?

_____

_____

_____

_____

_____

_____

_____

_____

_____

_____

_____

_____

_____

_____

_____

3
Low Self-Esteem

I don't think I've ever struggled with something as much more than low self-esteem. And I was aware that I had low self-esteem based on how I would allow others to treat me. I have been through the ringer with men. Emotional abuse was very common. Manipulation was very common. Disrespect to my body was very common. And it's as if the more people I *thought* I loved disrespected me, the more I fought to be seen by them. I had no boundaries with people. I came up with every excuse in the book why I should keep certain guys around, and often blamed or tried to change myself when I saw that they were mistreating me. It was as if the little girl Kia, the one who sought to hear simple things such as "I love you" from her Dad had taken over my mind and body.

I thought that maybe if I aligned myself to be everything they wanted me to be, they would treat me better. They would finally choose me. But it NEVER happened and rightfully so. I wasn't being my authentic self.

Later I would learn that I was always enough.

5.17.2019

A Love Letter To You

>Maybe it started in childhood.
>
>Maybe you can't quite pinpoint the moment where someone or something made you feel that your minor flaws were too much for someone else. Maybe that's when you allowed yourself not to be handled with care.
>
>If that's the case, then understand that it happens. We are all merely works in progress when it comes to this journey of self-love.
>
>Dating can be exhausting.
>
>And bogus.
>
>And downright irritating as fuck.
>
>And yet, you desire to be connected with someone. You desire to come home and have someone you can bounce ideas off of at night.
>
>You have a desire to be loved -- not in fragments like they've been doing, but fully. In whole. Cuz you're a whole lotta woman and you deserve someone who is up for the task.
>
>Maybe you know this, but you self-sabotage to avoid getting too close to anybody.
>
>Getting hurt quite often can do that, can't it?
>
>Trust me, I understand. And I can't say melting your heart to let someone else in will be easy.. And sometimes it will feel as if it's not worthwhile.

But what if I told you that you were more than your trauma? What if I told you that you were more than your heartbreak?

What if I told you that there is another side to love, one that doesn't include the battle wounds or scars that you've endured in your past?

What if I told you that your past doesn't even matter? What matters right now is the present and all the things you're doing in it.

You're amazing. I don't think you hear that often.

I hope that one day, you don't subject yourself to searching for yourself in the arms of broken men.

I hope that one day, you choose peace over the chaos you've become accustomed to.

We all deserve somebody.

Even when we think we are too flawed and fucked up to date.

Peace and love,

Kia

How has your self-esteem played a role in you practicing (or not practicing) self-love?

_____
_____
_____
_____
_____
_____
_____
_____
_____
_____
_____
_____
_____
_____
_____
_____

If you have low self-esteem, what made you develop it?

If you have high self-esteem, how did you develop it?

4
Self-Sabotage

Once a person gets their self-esteem high, you must then deal with self-sabotage that often peeks in the shadows right after.

I was a habitual self-sabotager. I had a hard time believing that after years of chaos and dysfunction, peace was my new normal. To be honest, being normal scared me. I self-sabotaged some chances at healthy relationships and often went back to the same things that caused me great pain.

I didn't recognize myself a lot during this recurring time period. I had a routine down: Separate myself from certain people. Invite them back in. Get hurt. "Get over it". Repeat.

This went on for years. And years. I made the cycles so hard to break because…. Well, I simply didn't want to. Online, I preached a good game about letting people go who couldn't treat you like you deserve to be treated but behind closed doors, I was a mess. And I was addicted to that mess and I welcomed that mess.

My last act of self-sabotage made me write a letter to myself after the smoke and mirrors cleared. I remember feeling so embarrassed. And frustrated. And emotionally exhausted. People often say that to do the same thing over and over again yet expect different results, is a sign of insanity.

And maybe…. Maybe I was insane. Or at least it felt like I was going that way.

I was upset with myself for allowing someone I had a trauma bond with back in my bed. I had been doing all this work in therapy, just to turn around and fuck a man that didn't deserve me. I ain't mad at him, but damn that was stupid.

Sometimes, we are our own worst enemies. A lot of us are not dumb, we are just accustomed to dysfunction so we just make it apart of our identities, getting further and further away from our best selves.

10.16.2019

Dear Kia,

> Of course I love you but I am currently disappointed in you.
>
> You know better.
>
> You make shit harder than what it needs to be. You act like some beast who can't be tamed, but the truth is, you don't wanna be tamed. You already know all your actions come with a consequence.
>
> You have already been down this road, this river, this creek before.
>
> Stop trying to make people be who you want them to be.
>
> Stop assigning people the wrong roles in your life. I love you enough to call you out on your shit and hold you accountable to the change you so desperately seek.
>
> Or do you really not wanna change but you strive for it because it sounds good?
>
> Be real with yourself, cuz you can't keep repeating the same dumb ass cycles fool.
>
> And I say this with love.
>
> You are self-sabotaging and self-destructing again. And for whatttttttttt? Cuz you wanted to feel something? Cool, but why from HIM?
>
> Do better.
>
> You deserve it, whether you think you do or not.

How are you your own worst enemy?

Why do you think you self-sabotage?

5
Am I trauma bonding?

Have you ever had a person in your life that you felt like you couldn't leave alone or they couldn't leave you alone?

Have you ever had a person in your life that no matter how bad they have treated you, you always find yourself running back, allowing them back in?

Have you ever found yourself in intense break up and make up cycles with a person? The cycle is vicious, yet you feel addicted?

If the answer is yes to any of those questions, then it's likely that you and this someone are sharing a trauma bond.

For those still confused, trauma bonding is when you have an intense emotional bond with someone that is usually toxic. It's dependent on emotional abuse. It is similar to Stockholm syndrome, which is when a victim begins to have feelings of compassion towards their captor, even though that person has caused them great turmoil and pain. Trauma bonds are the reason why it's hard for many people who are in mentally, physically, or emotionally abusive relationships to leave.

And you can trauma bond with anyone, not just a romantic partner or someone that you've sex with. You can trauma bond with your parents, your friends, and other family members as well.

In the context of self-love, breaking a trauma bond can be difficult because sometimes that person who has caused us so much pain and turmoil feels like home to us. Maybe we are comfortable with them. But in the context of home: what if home for you was toxic and dysfunctional? What if the people in your home were emotionally unavailable and silenced your voice? What if the people in your home did not honor or validate your emotions? What if "home" was simply a place where they struggled with showing affection and expressing their emotions in a healthy manner?

If that is the case for any of you reading this, then it is no secret that you choose partners that reflect "home." In a sick and twisted way, these trauma bonds make us feel safe because they feel like home.

Trauma bonding has kept me in situations that clear thinking and discernment would have had me avoid altogether. It has ripped me apart mentally, physically, and emotionally. I have been that person who couldn't seem to let plenty of someone's go and turned into a woman that went against everything I stood for.

One day, the mask fell off and I experienced something that could only be described as the straw that broke the camel's back.

I was lost. I was broken. I shed a layer of myself that had me feeling like a drug addict going through withdrawals.

I never knew how to break trauma bonds. I just knew that I had to, because constantly going through the same cycles over and over again was becoming life or death for me. In a previous chapter I said that sometimes we are our own worst enemies. At this point, I was tired of going to war with myself.

From there, I had to heal because I knew I wanted to become my best self, but couldn't do so in the current state of mind I was in.

There is something that me and all the women in my

immediate, extended, and chosen family all have in common: stories of heartache and pain. Stories of toxic relationships and codependency issues. Stories of soul ties. Stories of emotional abandonment. Stories of healing.

Trauma has a way of making you forget who you are, yet stay stagnant in your situation because you are too afraid to believe that you are worthy of better and while another person *could* give you better, the best person to give you better is always you. Therapy helped me realize that I would keep meeting the same person over and over again in different bodies until I healed the part of me that kept choosing them.

The journey of self-love is not linear, but it is a choice. For the longest, I struggled with choosing me. I always put the wellbeing of others above mine, because I wanted my voids filled, ego stroke, and space to avoid doing the inner work I knew I needed to do.

But life doesn't work like that. You can't escape the work.

What trauma bonds do you need to break?

What generational curses run in your family?

6
Accountability

It is easy to blame other people and the environment we grew up in, for why we end up in certain predicaments. For the longest, I avoided my own role in my own misery. I blamed other people and avoided the truth about myself until I had no choice but to face the mirror.

In a therapy session, my therapist gave me some homework after I shared that I was tired of meeting the same men over and over again, but in different bodies. All the men I've experienced may have looked physically different but they all had some things in common.

My therapist listened and gave me the assignment of answering these 3 questions:

- Why were certain men attracted to me?
- What messages about myself was I putting out towards these men?
- Why was I constantly *choosing* these types of men?

At the end of the day, *everything* is a choice. As a woman, *all types* of people will be attracted to me, so it is up to me to decide whether or not I want to engage with them.

Accountability is acknowledging that for every negative dating experience that I've had, I also had a role in it. Sometimes you have to ask yourself:

- Were there red flags I ignored?
- Were there boundaries I overstepped with people, or

boundaries that I let people overstep with me?

- Was I not honoring myself by letting others disrespect my body, my feelings, and my overall well-being as a person?

When the answer became yes to all or most of those questions, I knew then that I couldn't just blame other people anymore. I had a role in this shit too, and I needed to make a change.

But change…. Change is slow, change is gradual. Change happens in the mind first.

Fact about me: I am hard headed. I remember one of my decisions put me in the same boat that I always used to get in and how angry I was with myself. Many times during this self-love journey, I've stood face to face with the question: Do I deserve the love, peace, and happiness that I am seeking?

The answer is yes. But for some reason, I struggle(d) with believing it.

I think cultivating the love, peace, and happiness that is rightfully mine starts with better decision making, and better decision making starts with accountability. While it's okay to restart as many times as you need to, imagine if your decision making got better so you wouldn't have to press restart so many times?

Imagine the peace.

Imagine the harmony.

Imagine your soul being at ease.

Especially if you've already learned that lesson before, there would no longer be a need to self-inflict pain on yourself and constantly repeat it.

What is it that you *know* you deserve?

When you make decisions that can harm you, how can you hold yourself accountable to make sure you don't make those decisions again?

Name 3-5 things you won't allow yourself to do anymore that betrays your boundaries:

7
Healing

7.14.2019

Dear Kia,

Healing is not an overnight process, nor does it have to look like anyone else's journey. Healing requires work and sometimes isolation, but do not disappear without reflecting, analyzing, and applying what you've learned. I love you because your wisdom is infinite and you are fearless. You look at the discomfort of change in the face and still strive to do and be better anyway. I admire you for breaking up with self-sabotage and trauma. You have a newfound zest for life that makes me feel warm inside. I love you cuz you keep trying. You inspire me to keep trying too, no matter how tough it gets.

Love always,

Kia

Sometimes, I like to think of myself as a Phoenix, you know the one that has been through hell and back yet rises from the same ashes that were meant to kill her? Yeah, that's me.

Healing feels like it will kill me at times and to be honest with you, I don't always want to do it.

I don't always want to be my best self.

But I know I have to.

This journey is mine and no one else's. Because of this, the journey is also lonely and scary too. This journey is confusing and a whole lotta work. Despite all of this, I know that healing is not impossible for me and I know that I am healing at the right pace.

For a long time, I tried to rush my healing process. Imagine being a person who went from not acknowledging my hurt and pain to refusing to process it. Imagine breezing through trauma as if it never happened.

But it happened.

I've been hurt.

I've been broken.

I've been lost.

I had to rebuild myself.

And I am still rebuilding myself.

Healing is my sole responsibility, so I have to put in this work. No one else can do it.

Some days, I feel really powerful going through this healing process.

Other days, I feel as if Imma always be hurting.

Do you ever truly get over things? Or do you just simply grow from it, and remember the lessons?

What about us in the in-between? Meaning, those of us who are no longer actively hurting but still ain't fully healed? What is it that we do? It feels like being trapped between 2 worlds. How do we break free from it?

Lately I've been asking myself: Kia, do you wanna heal or do you wanna be distracted?

The truth was, I wanted to be distracted. I didn't want to heal because I did not know who I was outside of recurring drama and toxicity. Distracting myself kept me from diving into those deep, dark, feelings.

Distraction helped me go through the motions of life.

Healing required too much self-reflection.

Healing isn't what it looked like in the movies, but I wanted it to be so bad.

But, everyone must do their own work. Healing was my responsibility and my responsibility only.

Yesterday, I chose distraction.

Today, I choose to heal.

What does your healing process look like for you?

How do you know when you're healing vs. being distracted?

In what ways are you doing your own work?

Compared to when you first started your self-love journey to now,

How have you grown in self-love?

_____

_____

_____

_____

_____

_____

_____

_____

_____

_____

_____

_____

_____

_____

_____

8
Am I Doing This Right?

What does healing the right way, even look like?

For a while, I wanted to know the answer to that and tried my hardest to mimic an unrealistic formula on how healing was supposed to go. But if I've learned anything on this journey, it's that there is no right way or wrong way to heal and healing isn't linear anyway.

Some days will be harder than others and that's okay.

There isn't a timeline to heal, though some days we feel like we are back tracking.

But I assure you, you are healing yourself at the right pace.

You are in competition with no one but yourself and you are the one who makes the rules for this shit.

No one else but you.

So as you read this, breathe easy. Sleep a little better at night knowing that with the current tools that you have, you are doing the best you can. And doing the best you can while becoming a better version of yourself each day is what matters the most.

As for me and my journey, I have become less concerned with doing this right and more concerned with doing this authentically.

One day, I'll look up and shit won't always be like this. And it will be because I picked up my pieces and shed my layers in the most authentic way possible, without ever stressing myself out about if I'm doing this right.

Do you think there is a right or wrong way to heal? Why or Why not?

What does healing authentically mean to you?

9
What if I never find my person?

12.25.2019

Dear Kia,

As the holiday passes and you observe people who share their declaration of love for each other, your heart aches for that.

Jokingly, you wonder what your life would be like if you had settled for that married man. Or the man who never valued you. Or the man who took advantage of you. Or the man who wanted to change you.

What would your life be like if you had settled for less than what you deserved?

You wouldn't be happy.

You wouldn't be emotionally well. What about the risk your body would've gone through?

You know it's not worth it. And you know you don't have to receive answers to your questions, cuz you know.

You know not to settle.

You know that even though you're lonely, it's better than settling for crumbs at the bottom.

You know you wouldn't want to be sent a partner to cure your loneliness, cuz you know that you deserve a partner for way more than that.

You know exactly what you want and even though it makes you anxious if you'll actually receive that or not, you know you won't settle for anything less.

Stay true to you, because the work you do to know and revel in your worth is not in vain.

Love,

Kia

Sometimes I feel like the universal self-love message goes like this: If you work on yourself enough, heal completely, etc. then you'll find someone who appreciates you and all the work you've put in. It's like once you find your person, then your self-love journey is complete -- because you've found your person. And that's why we're doing all this work anyway right?

Wrong.

While there is nothing wrong with wanting to heal ourselves so we can attract healthier relationships in the future, our self-love journeys do not stop once we get into a relationship.

Furthermore, what if we never find our person? What if we are meant to stay single and not experience long term, romantic partnership? Does this mean that the work we put in is pointless now?

Truly, *why* are we practicing self-love?

Those are questions that keep me up at night. I've spoken about my fears and anxiety of being forever single extensively in therapy. I long for healthy, long term partnership and babies. But the question still lingers at the back of my mind, what if I NEVER find MY person?

I fear being that extremely successful woman yet her love life is either chaotic or just quiet and non-eventful. My degrees can't keep me warm at night. I can work hard as hell and accomplish thing after thing, but that doesn't take away from the loneliness. And sure, I have love from my friends and family, but self-love does not replace my desire for a healthy relationship rooted in authenticity, trust, healing, and love.

As much chaos, trauma, and turmoil I have experienced, a part of me sees a healthy romantic relationship as some sort of reward for all this self-love I've been practicing.

But…. It's not a reward.

Because regardless if I find my person or not, I still deserve love, respect, kindness, joy, and authenticity. These are things that I can give myself but these are things that I also intentionally seek out in a person.

My self-love isn't based on whether or not someone is able to see me or not.

My self-love sets the standard for how I expect and demand to be treated.

My self-love saves my life.

My self-love reminds me that I do not have to settle and that I have the power to change my normal anytime I want.

Why are you practicing self-love?

How do you combat loneliness while practicing self-love?

What do you deserve out of your relationships?

What do you intentionally look for?

_____

_____

_____

_____

_____

_____

_____

_____

_____

_____

_____

_____

_____

_____

_____

What do you think it says about you if you never find your person?

_____
_____
_____
_____
_____
_____
_____
_____
_____
_____
_____
_____
_____
_____
_____
_____

10
Redefining Self-Love

10.7.2019

Dear Kia,

It is easy to get stuck on the loneliness of celibacy and singleness but please remember that peace of mind is better than chaos. Please remember that you are creating a new normal and that your life is not boring now just because you no longer invite dysfunction into it. You are a pure soul with a gentle heart and you deserve to experience a love that does not require suffering first.

You know by now that emotional distress does not equate to love and is not the type of energy you want to bring into your future partnership. You deserve a lover and to give yourself a love that does not require you to compromise your mental health, just to say you got somebody.

I know it's scary out there…. You are paranoid that peace and serenity is nothing but a scam and that is why you may retreat back into past behaviors.

I don't judge you. I have become more gentle in loving you, but I will still hold you accountable.

Pressing forward with self-love no matter how scary the unknown is, is a true act of fearlessness.

And if I know anything about you, I know you won't let yourself be scared too long of shit.

I love you and I want you to approach each day with the mantra that peace is better than chaos.

No more suffering, all love from here on out.

Love,

Kia

10.25.2019

Dear Kia,

> The moment you let it go was the moment your power within expanded.
>
> You were always a powerful being to me, and you always had the strength to make your feet move.
>
> You are fearless when it comes to speaking up for yourself.
>
> You are triumphant in walking away.
>
> I am in awe of you, but not surprised. You've always had this in you.
>
> I am proud of you.
>
> I love you, for loving you.
>
> I love you, for trusting you.
>
> I love you, for believing in you.
>
> You are sooooo powerful.
>
> Love,
>
> Kia

If you would've asked me 4 years ago what were my thoughts and feelings on self-love, I would have simply said: *"love yourself or nobody will."*

What a limited world view I had. How can something like self-love, which is so personal, be reduced down to loving yourself or no one will? I'm not sure where the phrase came from but I for one, know it's not true.

First of all, people love people who don't love themselves *all* the time.

The respect may not be there and the love may not last long, but there isn't a shortage of being loved by others just because you don't love yourself.

My other issue with the phrase is, why is our self-love journey based on other people and their approval?

Loving yourself shouldn't even be based on whether or not someone will love you back.

As I said in an earlier chapter, even if you never find your person for your romantic fairytale ending, it does not mean your self-love journey is in vain.

Self-love as I know it is more than just memes and quotes. It's a real life practice that involves reprogramming your brain. It is sitting with yourself, unpacking why you accept certain treatment, why you choose certain partners, why chaos seems to be so embedded in you.

Self-love is accountability. Do your choices in people reflect the standards that you have set for yourself? Do you even know what your standards are in the first place?

Self-love is about forgiving yourself. You've learned this lesson already, why are you making yourself repeat it?

Self-love is not just for men, not just for women, but for everyone. The community. The world.

The world needs to heal itself, so we can create a better future. For ourselves, our children, our legacies.

The deeper you go within your self-love journey, you will learn that you need community.

Community can offer support, resources, a listening ear, whatever you may need-- just to show you that you are not alone and we are all journeying through this thing together.

My self-love journey is now a living testament to who I am becoming as a woman. It honors that little girl I once was, who healed her hurt and preps her as a woman of the future. I now know that I deserve peace, respect, consistency, and healthy love.

I know now that just because I may have witnessed unhealthy relationships and marriages growing up, does not mean that those same patterns will be my fate. I now know that I have the power to create myself a new normal (shout out to therapy for that one.)

I know now that I do not have to jump through hoops to win the affection of anyone. I know that self-love does not replace my yearning for romantic love, but it sure as hell does help me set my standards, hold myself accountable, and ex out anyone that doesn't measure up.

I now know that I don't have to self-sabotage or self-sacrifice just for a temporary thrill in hopes of getting a longer one.

I may not be 100% good at it, but I now know what it

means to love myself. And I hope by reading this, you start your journey too.

Love,

Kia

Do you have any fears when it comes to self-love?

Is the word "toxic" overused in relationships?

How do you know when a relationship is toxic?

What feelings have you experienced while on your self-love journey?

If you want kids or if you have kids, what do you want to teach them about self-love?

How are you redefining your self-love journey?

11
Your Turn

Now that you've journeyed with me, I want you to journey with you. When this challenge first started, I had people posting pictures of themselves followed by the words they wanted to use in their letter. It was easy for some, but much harder for others. Some people aren't used to affirming themselves. Some people never grew up having life spoken into them. Some people never took the time to self-reflect and figure out why they act or react the way that they do.

Some people feel as if they are broken beyond repair. And I weep for those people, because it isn't true. I truly believe that no matter how much you have been through, you have the power to love yourself and your self-love can heal you. There is so much salvation in it.

It just starts with belief.

Followed by action.

Then consistent practice.

None of us will be perfect at it.

And consistency and accountability develops over time.

But it starts with pushing past the fear, and believing.

As you begin your letter to yourself, I want you to center yourself. Go to wherever your quiet place is and think: What do you love about you? What are you proud of? What have you overcome? Even if it's the smallest thing, put it in your letter. My hope is that this becomes a consistent practice for you, that you become comfortable in writing to yourself, that you become confident in it.

How you feel about yourself sets the tone for everything else in your life. How you treat yourself, teaches people how to treat you. Learn to love yourself, like your life depends on it.

Because it does.

Dear _____,

Love,

How does it feel writing a love letter to yourself?

Was it easy? Was it hard? What emotions came up for you?

Epilogue

To the 12-year-old I once was, Who cried because she wanted a boyfriend.

Who once questioned if she was good enough.

Pretty enough.

Worthy enough.

You are free now.

About the Author

Kia Smith is a multifaceted writer, award nominated journalist, and relatable real life blogger who resides on the South Side of Chicago.

As a self-described dramatic and emotional child, Kia found solace and space to express her creativity in writing, and has been sharing her thoughts and feelings in the digital space for over a decade, gaining notoriety for her relatable content and authentic voice.

All throughout her time at Harlan High School, she filled up notebooks and magazines with her thoughts and even had a successful YouTube series where she perfected her journalism skills. She then took her talents to Southern Illinois University in Carbondale, where she continued to sharpen her creativity through blogging while gaining professional experience as a student journalist.

Years removed from college, Kia is now in her late twenties, trying to survive adulting and inspiring people with her stories, one book at a time.

Connect with Kia on her most used social media platforms.

Instagram: @KiaSmithWrites

Twitter: @KiaSmithWrites_

Email: kiasmithwrites@gmail.com

Website: www.kiasmithwrites.com

Scan below for social media sites

www.ingramcontent.com/pod-product-compliance
Lightning Source LLC
Chambersburg PA
CBHW051445290426
44109CB00016B/1678